Introduction

Every class in Ireland was affected in some way by the catastrophe of 1845-50. Even before the second cycle of crop failure and epidemic in 1848-9, it helped bring about a fundamental change in Irish land law: the Famine having stretched to financial breaking-point many already indebted landlords, the first Encumbered Estates Act became law in 1848, followed by a more radical one in 1849. These were designed drastically to simplify the transfer of landed property, allowing debtors to sell their estates more easily, and investors in Ireland and England (who had supposedly been shy of entering the legal maze of Irish land purchase) to acquire Irish estates with secure title. To some this legislation promised a new rural social order.

The first actual survey of Irish rural society in the aftermath of the Famine was the Census of 1851, which included comprehensive agricultural statistics for that year. Most people, according to the Census Commissioners, still lived in the countryside (83 per cent), and the families of the 570,338 tenant farmers enumerated accounted for over half of the rural population. The bulk of the remainder were landless labourers — either servants living with their masters, or precariously supporting their families as 'outdoor' labourers. A third group, almost insignificant numerically, was the landlords, who owned most of the land and numbered at most 10,000. The history of the next half century was to be dominated by the ferment in relations between landlords, tenants and labourers, and by the changing economic status of each group within agriculture.

Over a quarter of the country's surface was tilled in 1851, producing cereals, root crops and hay — only potatoes had declined dramatically from pre-Famine levels. In 1851 the agricultural economy was apparently still in a state of crisis: the potato had lost its potency, low agricultural prices gave little promise of recovery to those who had survived, and the now

3

slightly larger holdings hardly made up for the greatly increased poor-law rates.

From the 1850s on, however, change was rapid: livestock increased in value and numbers, tillage declined slowly, and a prosperous stability was enjoyed by the tenant farmers, whose numbers remained relatively stable for the next fifty years. Landless labourers declined dramatically from over 700,000 in 1851 to just under 260,000 in 1901. By the end of the century there were fewer people in rural Ireland but they were better off, and tenant farmers accounted for a significantly larger proportion of the whole. A useful indicator of the importance of tenant farmers in rural society (and of their prosperity) was the growing proportion of the rural population living in relatively good houses: only 17 per cent lived in houses with 5 or more rooms in 1841, 27 per cent in 1851, and 56 per cent in 1901.

The value of agricultural output in the 1850s was in the region of £35 millions. Rent payments absorbed more than 28 per cent (or just over £10 millions) of this, and the two largest groups in the rural population, farmers and labourers, shared the remaining 71 per cent, or just under £25 millions. The landlords owned the land, letting it to tenants in amounts ranging from small strips of less than an acre to large farms of perhaps 2,000 acres. The land was occupied by the tenants, and worked by them and their labourers. The distinct roles of landlords, tenants and labourers, while conforming neatly to the contemporary distinction between land, labour and capital as the factors of production, did not prevail everywhere in unmitigated simplicity. First, many landlords were farmers in their own right, retaining large demesnes and home farms around their houses; demesne land probably accounted for not less than 15 per cent of Ireland's 20,000,000 acres. Secondly, the distinction between tenants and labourers did not conform to the classical distinction between labour and capital as factors of production, because many farmers were labourers in the sense that they worked their own farms, earning wages as well as profits. Any attempt, therefore, to estimate the amount of agricultural output shared by the three groups must take into account these overlappings. The landlords probably earned about £12 millions, including the profits of demesne farming; the landless labourers, assuming that most received a typical year's wages, probably earned £9 millions; the balance, about £14 millions, represented the tenants' profits and wages.

The contrast between landlords and tenants was great. Many landlords had enormous estates: the Duke of Leinster had 73,000 acres in Kildare and Meath, the Marquis of Downshire had 115,000 in five counties, and the Duke of Abercorn, one of the few great Irish landlords to serve as Lord Lieutenant of Ireland in the mid-nineteenth century, had 76,000 acres in Donegal and Tyrone. Even the typical landlord, although he did not compare with these titled leviathans, probably had about 2,000 acres; a survey of estates in the 1870s showed that 20 per cent of the country was owned by landlords with estates ranging from 2,000 to 5,000 acres, and over half the country was owned by less than a thousand great landlords. Irish tenants' holdings were by contrast relatively small, being on average about 40 acres; the typical tenant, however, had even less than 40 acres—in 1851 over half of them had less than 15 acres.

The starkness of the contrast can of course be exaggerated: there was a numerous class of small landlords who were important in their localities as resident gentry, but who were not very different from large farmers. Also, some tenants were substantial men: Edward Delany of Woodtown in County Meath, for example, with his 500 acres, his shares in the Midland Great Western Railway, and his gig, was a substantial figure compared with some small landlords. One of the paradoxes of Irish rural society was that while most tenants were small and most estates large, much of the actual area of the country was occupied by large tenant farmers. In 1861, for example, 40 per cent of the country was held in farms of 100 acres and over—Ireland was a country of large farms and small farmers.

There can be little doubt, then, about the economic power of Irish landlords in the post-Famine period. Even the typical Irish landlord was wealthier than all but the grandest of Prussian junkers; as a class, with a specific, definable source of income, they were a formidable group, with a collective income that was more than the public revenue of Ireland and more than the cost of maintaining the Royal Navy. Since the rental of over £10 millions was distributed among a relatively small group, they were one of the best-paid vested interests in the British empire — the great coal owners and Indian maharajas excepted. There is a danger, however, in assuming that such landed wealth meant that landlords were the sole or even the major agents of economic change. Certainly they were still perceived to be controlling the engine of economic and social change, speeding it up by removing useless tenants; slowing it down by neglect; or determining the efficiency of land use by charging realistic rents. But, as we shall see, times were changing.

Their formal political power, that is the power they wielded through offices conferred on them by tradition and status, was also still impressive in the 1850s: they acted as justices of the peace, as *ex officio* poor-law guardians, as county grand jurors, and as managers and patrons of schools. Their informal political power is shown by their continuing dominance of parliamentary politics: in 1852, 68 of Ireland's 104 M.P.s were from landed families, and in all elections up to 1880 landlord influence played an important part in returning candidates — both liberal and conservative. Their strength in Parliament was greater than their numbers might suggest, for they were able to ally with the powerful landed interest in Britain.

The 'land question' was not, however, a controversy over the wealth of landlords, or their political power. Initially at least, it concerned specific aspects of the relationship between them and their tenants. Defined narrowly as landlord-tenant relations, the 'land question' assumed a much greater role in Irish affairs in the 1850s, replacing repeal of the Union as a major electoral issue in the general election of 1852 (a measure of the impact of the new Tenant League, founded in 1850). Although it was fashionable in the late nineteenth century to see the land question as the product of a long historical process going back to the seventeenth-century confiscations, it really only emerged in a specific form in the 1840s and early 1850s, embracing the issues of free trade in landed property, the operation of the Encumbered Estates Acts, and above all 'the three Fs' (fair rent, freedom of sale of tenancy, and fixity of tenure). These issues persisted and influenced the Land Acts of 1860 and 1870, were the specific economic issues of the Land War of 1879-82, and were taken into account in the Land Act of 1881, which conceded 'the three Fs', and in the Arrears Act of 1882. For the next forty years governments — Conservative and Liberal, British and Irish — struggled to dismantle landlordism on terms attractive to both landlords and tenants, finally abolishing landlordism in the Free State in 1923 and in Northern Ireland in 1925. In a certain sense 'the land question' was perennial, preceding the nineteenth century's preoccupation with 'tenant right', and surviving the abolition of traditional landlordism in the 1920s: but the substance of the actual 'question' changed, for confiscation in the seventeenth century was as different from 'the three Fs', as they are from butter mountains and farmers' liability to pay income tax.

Within the period dominated by the purely tenurial land question — roughly from the appointment of the Devon commission in 1843 to the Northern Ireland Land Act, 1925 — there were long periods of social and political tranquillity, almost of indifference, punctuated by periods of intense debate and conflict: the early 1850s, 1869-70, 1879-82 and 1886-91. Although these episodes have a special attraction for historians, if only because they provide much needed markers in an apparently formless landscape, the period 1848-78 as a whole is of crucial importance. It was during these thirty years that ideas were formed, solutions proposed, and political dispositions made or planned; in the much longer period from 1878 to 1925, the pattern was more firmly set, and there were fewer options for landlords, tenants and governments. Above all, during the period 1848-78 landlords had a chance to succeed, the Encumbered Estates Acts having swept away insolvent landlords, and agricultural prosperity from the mid-1850s giving landlords room to manœuvre; the groups that would eventually challenge the landlords' power were before the late 1870s either in disarray, otherwise engaged, or simply unorganized.

The land question has always been a major preoccupation of historians, but it has probably attracted more attention during the last fifteen years than at any time since the nineteenth century. In the 1930s J. E. POMFRET, Elizabeth HOOKER, and N. D. PALMER elaborated rather than challenged the nineteenth-century tradition of predatory landlordism. POMFRET and HOOKER assumed that positive law influenced most human behaviour; that landlords had rackrented and evicted frequently because the law had allowed them to do so; that tenants had been deterred from improving their holdings because they feared eviction and rackrents and because the law gave them no compensation when they quitted their holdings; and that as a result the Irish countryside had been poor and endemically violent: attacks on landlords and agents had been frequent, and the failure of both landlords and tenants to invest in improvements had impoverished agriculture. These ideas, somewhat simplified, found their way into popular histories and school textbooks, largely sustained by a lively folk tradition of predatory landlordism. In Christopher Preston's *A School History of Ireland, pt. ii, 1607-1949* (Dublin, n.d.), the prelude to the Land War of 1879 was presented simply as a worsening of the land system: 'Since the Famine, the position of the tenants had got worse. There were more evictions than ever . . . . Rackrents evictions and clearances were the rule' (pp 116-17).

In the 1960s attention was again attracted to the land question, partly by the new availability of primary sources such as estate papers, and partly by two interesting works: Raymond CROTTY's *Irish Agricultural Production,* which cast doubt on the economic advantages of peasant proprietary, and by implication endorsed the old landlord system; and R. D. C. BLACK's *Economic Thought and the Irish Question 1817-1870,* which showed the powerful intellectual foundations that maintained the *laisser-faire* system of landlord-tenant relations until 1870 and inspired the Encumbered Estates Acts and the Land Acts of 1860. From the 1960s research has advanced steadily: Olive ROBINSON's 1962 essay on the London companies in County Londonderry; B. L. SOLOW's *The Land Question and the Irish Economy, 1870-1903* in 1971; J. S. DONNELLY's *The Land and the People of Nineteenth-Century Cork* in 1974; W. E. VAUGHAN's 1977 general essay on landlords and tenants; and L. P. CURTIS's recent article on landlord indebtedness. Coinciding with an interest in landlords and tenants is a growing interest in the Land War, represented by Paul Bew's *Land and the National Question* (1978) and Samuel Clark's *Social Origins of the Irish Land War* (1979).

Reconciling the new research that has been published from the 1960s with the apparent verdict of history is not easy. New sources, and to a lesser extent, new techniques of analysis give the new ideas an exactness not found in Hooker and Pomfret; remoteness from the events themselves has bred a certain detachment; the land question's role in the development of nineteenth-century politics is clearer simply because more is known about politics. Yet it is hard to believe that the last word has been said, if only because the issues that have preoccupied historians — rents, evictions, tenant right and agrarian crime — are only the skeleton, or outline, of a whole system of social relationships. In the meantime, however, these subjects remain a central concern and the old questions receive new answers: were rents high and evictions frequent? were agrarian crimes important? what was tenant right? what caused the land war? why did landlordism fail? Before we examine these questions further, we must try to appreciate the limitations of landlord power, even in the generation before the land war.

THE LIMITS OF LANDLORD POWER

On the face of it, the law gave very considerable freedom to landlords in how they dealt with their tenantry. The most common agricultural contract was the yearly tenancy, which could be terminated with only six months' notice to quit; the rent could, in theory, be increased every year, and evicted tenants had no claims to compensation for improvements until the passing of the Land Act of 1870. Before 1870 a determined landlord could not only evict his tenants in a very short time, but he could do it without risking any pecuniary loss. One of the most publicized clearances of the post-Famine period was the evictions at Derryveagh, Co. Donegal: in November 1860 notices to quit that had been served ten months previously expired; the tenants gave up legal possession to allow their farms to be rearranged, but they were actually left *in situ;* in February 1861, the landlord, John George Adair, having decided that his tenants were involved in the murder of his steward, James Murray, proceeded to enforce the ejectments; on 8-10 April, therefore, just over a year since the initiation of the legal proceedings against the tenants, 47 families were evicted by the sub-sheriff of Donegal.

The law did not however give landlords privacy in their dealings with tenants, nor did the great estates conceal their wealth and power. The landlords' houses and demesnes were grandly impressive; estates were concentrated in great territorial blocks; tenants of the same landlord, unlike clients of the same bank, knew each other because of their palpable contiguity. All this helped to make the working of the tenurial relationship a public affair; and the twice-yearly collection of rents often took place in hotels or in specially built estate offices prominently located in country towns; evictions were carried out in public, often accompanied by sensational publicity. From the 1840s, there was an increasing body of information about landlords and tenants collected by the government, much of which was published: statistics concerning evictions, agrarian crimes, leases, absenteeism and rents, as well as the reports of select committees and royal commissions.

This expanding public interest paralleled the gradual intrusion of statutory regulation into landlord-tenant relations. Admittedly there was a tendency, culminating in the Land Acts of 1860, to enable landlords and tenants to make whatever agreement suited themselves, free of traditional or prescriptive obligations; but most tenants were yearly tenants, a form of tenancy presumed by law to exist in the absence of written agreements. In theory and often in practice, yearly tenants were harshly treated; nevertheless the law, even in the 1850s, gave them some protection. The landlord could not behave as he pleased; the tenancy could be changed or ended only by agreement between the landlord and tenant, or by legal action; the landlord could not, for example, simply remove the tenant by force—indeed there are examples of the police protecting tenants from illegal eviction. In fact the law presumed that a yearly tenancy would continue unchanged from year to year, unless ended by legal action or agreement. It did not end, consequently, every year at a certain date, like tenancies in Belgium where tenants could be required to leave on Christmas eve after only a few hours' notice. If a landlord wanted to get rid of a tenant, he had to end the tenancy by serving notice to quit. At every point, therefore, landlords were forced to use the law and to take part in public and protracted wrangles whose outcome was uncertain.

Contemporary critics of the landlord interest asserted that as the law permitted evictions and rackrenting, it could be assumed that they took place. The publicity surrounding landlord-tenant dealings provided many examples that supported the initial hostile premise, and to some extent the official compilation of eviction and agrarian crime statistics created a further misleading impression. If, for example, statistics of disputes between farmers and labourers had been compiled, it is certain that arbitrary dismissals would have exceeded evictions.

The new degree of public interest in the relationship created the impression that extreme behaviour was the norm and encouraged facile conclusions concerning the legal powers of landlords. In fact the law did not move decisively towards freedom of contract; the Land Acts of 1860 merely tidied up the existing system without abolishing the legal protection surrounding yearly tenancy. A complete legal *tabula rasa*, for example, would have left tenants no better off than caretakers who could be removed by *force majeure* — without rights of any kind. (The statute law in 1860 moved less sharply towards freedom of contract than it did in 1870 towards prescription.) Furthermore, the traditional distinction between civil and criminal law became, in practice, greater with the establishment of a police force; for the two were not assimulated in the nineteenth century, and the police did not enforce the law of landlord and tenant — they merely protected the sub-sheriff and his officers in the execution of their duties. If the new constabulary had been made directly responsible for serving ejectment processes, making distraints, executing civil bill decrees, a revolution in the landlord-tenant relationship would have taken place. Landlords themselves did little in the post-Famine period to transform the relationship with their tenants (with the possible exception of the notorious William Scully, a Tipperary landlord who was almost murdered in an affray with his tenants in 1868). They inherited a legalistic, visible and vulnerable system; it would have been in their own interests to have made it more secretive, less dependent on the courts, and less one-sided; great estates should have vanished behind land-management companies; even the tenurial relationship could have been transformed by systems of land purchase and mortgage repayments by instalments. The landlords in the eighteenth century had been the undisputed economic and legal centres of their localities; in the nineteenth century the state reduced them gradually to being merely rich men who lived in the countryside — their self-evident status by the early twentieth century. Their weakness was that they did not sufficiently reorganize the basis of their wealth to make that fact a comfortable one.

RENTS, EVICTIONS, CRIME AND TENANT RIGHT

The historiography of the Irish land question has been more concerned with tenurial problems — rents, evictions, tenant right and agrarian crime — than that of Britain (with the possible exception of Wales). POMFRET demonstrates this clearly in a summary of his views of the period between the Famine and the Land Act of 1870:

> By 1860 the power of the Irish landlord was at the zenith. He was enabled by law to dispose of his property as he saw fit. At the end of the current year the great mass of tenancies were legally terminated and there was no obligation binding him to continue the occupiers in possession. If it were desirable the landlord would make a new contract with the tenant, but if he saw fit he might cast him off. (pp 47-8)

There are understandable reasons for the continuing emphasis on tenurial problems. First, the political debate at the time was dominated by the tenurial question; secondly, the traditional picture of Irish landlordism, whether in POMFRET and HOOKER, in school textbooks, or in folklore, has been dominated by rackrenting and eviction. In retrospect there are perhaps more important issues, but the tenurial ones played such an important role that they were tackled first when historians began reassessing the land question in the 1960s and 1970s. When systematic research began, changes in interpretation came so quickly and so effectively that it became difficult to understand how the old ideas had such power. (One of the minor preoccupations of historians now is to find predatory landlords such as John George Adair, William Scully and the third earl of Leitrim.) The work of ROBINSON, DONNELLY and SOLOW seemed remarkable when it was published, for it challenged so many of the old verities; now it has among professional historians almost an air of *déjà vu*.

In assessing the tenurial system, historians faced two problems. First, to discover what actually happened; for example, the size of rent increases, the number of evictions and agrarian crimes, and the working of the tenant right custom; secondly, to evolve ways of measuring their significance. The

13

first was easier in the 1960s than it had been in the 1930s when POMFRET and HOOKER studied the land question, for considerable collections of manuscript estate papers had accumulated in public repositories such as the National Library of Ireland and the Public Record Office of Northern Ireland. The rentals showed, for example, that rackrenting had *not* been common; that rent increases were about 20 per cent on average between the Famine and the Land War; that many rents were not increased at all, and most only once. The rentals also showed how the other tradition might have been formed; for on most estates there were some apparently high rents, even though the average was low.

The rentals made accuracy possible; but they did more, for they enabled historians to reassess the great body of information contained in other sources such as the parliamentary reports and pamphlets, which had been the basis of POMFRET's work. Although POMFRET came to the conclusion that rackrenting was common, the great body of information in the sources he used suggests the opposite, for many witnesses testified to the moderation of rents. Why did POMFRET come to such a conclusion on the basis of his sources? It is impossible to answer this question with any accuracy, but there are two possible explanations. First, he accepted the verdict of history and merely tried to document it; secondly, it was easy to dismiss the contrary evidence, much of it emanating from landlords and agents, as tendentious, exceptional and *sui generis*. Good landlords existed, but they were exceptional; those who appeared before parliamentary enquiries spoke only for themselves, while the tenants' representatives spoke for the whole tenantry. POMFRET, in fact, exercised the caution that historians should exercise — but only in relation to part of his evidence. The fact that the opposite case could be constructed on the basis of the same evidence was demonstrated more recently in SOLOW's study, which relied heavily on the Bessborough commission and income tax returns — sources available to POMFRET.

The trouble with such literary evidence is that, because of its adversarial nature, it can be made to prove opposite arguments. Royal commissions, parliamentary inquiries and contemporary pamphleteers worked on the assumption that there were two sides to the question and that there was a problem to be disposed of; those who gave evidence did so because they had a point to make, or an axe to grind. (It is worth noting that the poor-law inspectors' reports presented to the government in 1870 give a more balanced picture, so balanced that they must have left Gladstone puzzled when he came to legislate — an unfortunate result of the inquisitorial as opposed to the adversarial procedure.) If parliamentary reports were the only sources, conclusions would be almost impossible: SOLOW, for example, could be dismissed as easily as she dismisses POMFRET. Also, given the strength of the tradition of bad landlordism in Ireland, some additional weight had to be added to such evidence favouring the landlord position, and the rentals gave that weight. The effect of the rentals was to show *why* so many contemporaries believed in rackrenting and why a general moderation in rent increases created so many anomalies; on most estates only individual rents were increased from time to time, thus creating stark contrasts in rent levels borne by neighbouring farmers. At any one time, some rents were high, some low and most moderate; but when they were exposed to public scrutiny, the high rents had the visibility of an iceberg's tip — and bore much the same relationship to the submerged mass.

The other tenurial problems have also been elucidated by a more detailed use of manuscript sources. Older information on evictions, for example, came mainly from police statistics (published as parliamentary papers), and judicial statistics compiled from court proceedings (published annually from 1864). There were two problems associated with these statistics. First, the evictions recorded by the police were fewer than the ejectment decrees granted by the courts; secondly, the police figures were presented without any explanation as to how they were compiled and of what the police regarded as an eviction. (Even the use of the word 'eviction' by the police, and the use of the word 'ejectment' by lawyers was puzzling). The estate papers helped to solve the first problem, for it appeared that threats of eviction greatly exceeded actual evictions, and tenants served with notices to quit or ejectment processes still appeared in the rentals years later. The discrepancy, therefore, between the two sets of figures was not only explained, but suggested that the *threat* of eviction was an important part of estate management.

The second historical problem was more complicated, and no help in solving it came from the estate papers. Did the police miss thousands of evictions through ignorance? Did they record only those where they were present to protect the sheriff? From what was known of the Irish constabulary, carelessness and ignorance seemed unlikely: there were plenty of police in the countryside to keep an eye on events; they attended the courts and had, therefore, advance warning of evictions; as collectors of statistics they were able and experienced, their greatest achievement in that field being the agricultural statistics of Ireland published annually from 1847. The solution to the problem was eventually found in the registered papers of the Chief Secretary's Office, where enough individual reports of evictions survive to show how the police worked. These reports show that the police counted all legal removals, including householders in towns as well as agricultural tenants; also they included all removals, regardless of the point in the legal process where they occurred — if tenants gave up possession when served with notice to quit, but before the courts sent the sheriff to eject them, the police counted that as an eviction; above all, it is clear that the police reported all evictions, even those where they were not required to be present to protect the sheriff. The 90,000 evictions returned between 1847 and 1880 are probably accurate; they certainly do not seriously underestimate the actual number; but they may exaggerate slightly if allowance is not made for town tenants and those tenants restored after eviction as caretakers, unknown to the police. The biggest eviction ever recorded by the police took place on the estates of Trinity College, Dublin, in 1851 when, according to the police, 753 families were evicted in Kerry. The Board of Trinity College has often been accused of oppression, but there is evidence that on this occasion the Board was innocent and that the evictions never took place. The letter-books of the Board are quite clear that no such evictions took place; the census returns for the district involved show no dramatic fall in population; and the valuation records show hundreds of tenants still *in situ* years later. What seems to have happened is that the Board evicted a large middleman tenant who had not paid his rent; the 753 families were his sub-tenants and were automatically evicted with him; but the procedure was a formality, and they were restored as tenants—but that fact was not fully recorded by the police.

Agrarian crime presents similar problems. Between 1848 and 1880 16,579 agrarian outrages were recorded by the police, including 206 homicides. These statistics and the sensational nature of some of the cases, such as the assassination of the third earl of Leitrim in 1878, created the impression that disorder was endemic in the Irish countryside. The very term 'agrarian outrage' implied that all of these were caused by landlord-tenant disputes; the *Oxford English Dictionary,* for example, defines agrarian crime as crime arising out of disputes between landlords and tenants. An analysis of actual cases, however, shows that the police defined all crimes arising out of disputes about land as agrarian, including family rows and disputes between neighbours. Of more than 100 agrarian homicides returned between 1858 and 1878, for example, only 24 per cent were caused by disputes between landlords and tenants. (Other studies confirm that only a fraction of agrarian crime was caused by landlord-tenant disputes: about 40 per cent, which is rather more than the homicides on their own would suggest, but still rather less than agrarian outrage statistics apparently suggest.)

'Tenant right' was less tangible than rents and evictions, and even than agrarian crime; it was 'a term of doubtful import', according to Mountifort Longfield, a judge of the Landed Estates Court and author of several articles on the land question. To some contemporaries, tenant right meant the three Fs; to others, it was compensation for improvements; to many it was a vague term meaning protection for tenants. Not even its territorial location was clear; it was often referred to as the Ulster custom of tenant right, but its operation does not seem to have been confined to Ulster; also there were estates in Ulster where the custom did not exist. Its importance, however, was great: it was

held up as a model to legislators, as it was supposed to guarantee
a better standard of landlord-tenant relations; and in Ulster and
some adjacent counties, whatever its vagueness, it was a reality
on most estates. And what was called 'tenant right' was given
legal status in 1870 in what must have been one of the shortest
but most important clauses ever inserted in a Victorian statute
regulating the rights of property.

Did tenant right before 1870 guarantee the three Fs, as
POMFRET believed? To some extent estate records help to clarify
the confusion created by the mass of contemporary comment
in parliamentary reports and pamphlets. It is absolutely clear,
for example, that tenants bought and sold something on Ulster
estates; on the Abercorn estates a list of sales, recorded by the
agent, shows large sums being paid by incoming tenants to their
predecessors: £563. 15s. in 1868, for example, for a small farm
on the Donegal estate, whose rent was only £15. On the Gosford
estates details of sales are also given, showing that the agent dealt
very carefully with them, trying to reconcile the conflicting claims
of heirs, widows, creditors and the landlord himself. (Also in
the Gosford papers there is a handbill advertising a sale and
referring to the tenant as the 'proprietor'.) The sums paid for
tenant right make one thing clear: the tenants were selling more
than the value of their improvements, for it is difficult to see
how improvements could have been worth so much. If the Duke
of Abercorn had sold his estate, he might have got twenty-two
times its annual rental; tenant right, in fact, was worth almost
as much.

If tenant right gave 'free sale', did it also give the other two
Fs? On these the estates papers are not so helpful; certainly few
tenants were evicted, even when in arrears; but it is clear in estate
correspondence that tenants could be evicted on Ulster estates,
even if they were not in arrears. What the custom did give the
evicted, however, was the right to sell their tenant right;
strictly speaking, therefore, Ulster tenants did not enjoy full fixity
of tenure, although it came close to it in practice. The question
of fair rents is much more difficult, for it is not clear how rents
were actually regulated on Ulster estates. Valuation, rather than
competition, was common, but it is impossible to be sure that

it was the practice on all estates. In any case, valuation did not necessarily guarantee 'fair' rents, for its results depended on how the valuators worked, and high rents could result. There is also the problem that rent increases were not lower in Ulster than in the rest of the country.

The problem of rents and tenant right can in fact only be solved by trying to discover why incoming tenants paid such large sums for farms that were held only on yearly tenancies, subject to substantial rents. According to contemporary economic theory, a yearly tenant had only a limited interest to sell: growing crops, possibly some improvements, and the convenience value of the unexpired term of the yearly tenancy. Although these might be substantial, they could hardly amount to half or three-quarters of the fee simple. The tenant's income was supposed to consist of wages for his labour and profits on his capital; rent was what he paid for the land, which can be best seen as a fodder-producing machine · hired by the tenant. Any large incoming payment, therefore, which exceeded a yearly tenant's rather limited interest, consumed part of the tenant's expected income from wages and profits; William Patton, on the Abercorn estate, who paid £340 for a farm in 1872, was sacrificing the equivalent of £13. 12s. a year, if it is assumed that contemporary rates of interest were about 4 per cent.

It is possible, even within contemporary economic theory, to discover reasons why incoming tenants would pay such large sums. A very small tenant, or labourer, might sacrifice his profits and wages just to enjoy the privilege of working for himself; even if a farm yielded nothing more than the equivalent of labourer's wages, it might be more attractive than working for someone else. A small farmer, without enough land to keep himself and his family fully employed, might buy land just to keep himself fully employed — so long as the return exceeded the ordinary interest that his money would earn, he was better off. Even a middling farmer might take land on disadvantageous terms to spread his overheads, especially the upkeep of horses; again there might be no profit in the strict economic sense, but the saving might make it worthwhile. There was also a sinister motive suggested by some contemporaries: the payment was blackmail, paid to prevent reprisals by the outgoing family. Doubtless all of these factors operated in some cases, although the last is highly dubious, for outgoing tenants were often widows, and a system based on blackmail would have been more erratic: farms vacated by male adolescent malcontents would have fetched more than those vacated by widows.

Yet hardly any of these considerations applied to large farmers who bought tenant right; why, for example, did a tenant in 1876 on the Abercorn estate pay £2,700 for a farm? There remains only one possible explanation: that the land was worth more than the rent charged.

Contemporaries often said that tenant right payments were like a second rent; but they were in fact part of the rent — the difference between what the landlord received and what the land was worth. In reality, purchasers were handing over a share of their future profits, and possibly wages, to the outgoing tenants; by the same token, the landlords could in theory have charged higher rents on sitting tenants. If tenant right was partially a capitalization of the uncollected rent, it followed that rent increases could reduce its value, and possibly even extinguish it completely — a shilling on the rent, said some contemporaries, took a pound off the tenant right. There was, therefore, a constant tension between rent and tenant right: tenant right could exist only if rents were 'fair' in the sense that they were less than the land was worth. Contemporaries spoke as if tenant right could be expressed as a series of rules regulating landlord-tenant relations; they had to, after all, if the custom was to be legalized; but the relationship was a dynamic one where two elements were in conflict. The conflict could only be resolved by sophisticated measurements involving prices, wages, interest rates and rents, which were not attempted, or whose necessity was not even recognized; even when such measurements were made, fundamental principles relating to the ownership of land would have had to be decided. Tenant right was much more complicated than the three Fs implied, and the mere legalization of the three Fs would have transformed it, and possibly even destroyed it.

CAN OPPRESSION BE MEASURED?

Having established that rents increased by about 20 per cent, that evictions rarely exceeded one for every 1,000 holdings in most years, that agrarian crime was a small fraction of total crime, and that tenant right was not the three Fs, how can historians evaluate their significance? Historical research may prove that the traditional picture of landlordism was exaggerated, but can it establish that the new, more accurate picture is not just a smaller dose of the old medicine? After all, if tenants were poor and agriculture was stagnating, a rent increase of 20 per cent would have been burdensome.

Rents are probably the easiest part of the tenurial relationship to assess. (They are also the most important since all tenants paid rent.) Between the 1850s and 1870s agriculture was not stagnating, but actually thriving because livestock markets were buoyant, especially in the mid-1850s and 1870s. Calculations of agricultural output show that by the mid-1870s it had increased by 47 per cent over the early 1850s average. Labour costs also increased — by about 50 per cent. Since rents increased by only 20 per cent, the tenants' share of agricultural output, whether wages or profits, increased dramatically; wages and profits combined increased by 62 per cent; profits on their own by a staggering 78 per cent. Actual rents collected between 1851 and 1880 amounted to £354 millions; if they had followed agricultural output, step by step, the total would have been £400 millions, or 13 per cent more. Such a system should not have been controversial since landlords and tenants would each have received a proportional share of the increased output. In 1851 Parliament passed an act to regulate rents on the estates of Trinity College, Dublin: initially the rents were fixed at a point determined by the government valuation, but arrangements were made, based on simple fractional calculations, to allow them to move upwards and downwards as agricultural prices fluctuated. If all land in Ireland had been let on this basis, total rents between 1851 and 1880 would have amounted to £442 millions,

FIGURE 1. AGRICULTURAL OUTPUT, LABOUR COSTS, AND RENTS, 1850-86

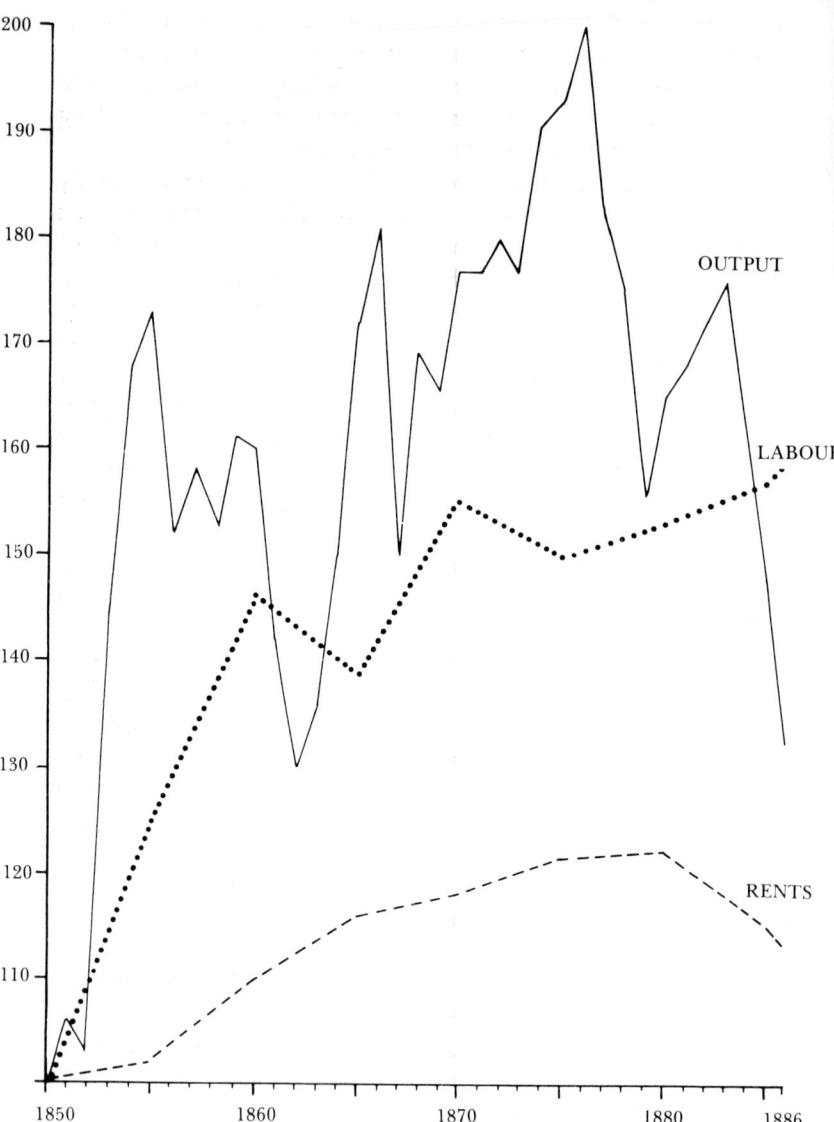

Based on calculations by the author, these curves show fluctuations at current prices from a base of 100 in 1850, when output was £25 millions, labour costs £11.5 millions, and rents £10.4 millions.

or 25 per cent above those actually received. As for rents, therefore, tenants were not only not rackrented, but did not even pay rents that would have been 'fair' by English standards. On the whole, tenants were in a relatively privileged position, holding their land at what were in real terms falling rents.

The 90,000 evictions between 1847 and 1880 are not so easily disposed of, especially the 50,000 that occurred during the years 1847-50: no calculations can mitigate the miserable plight of those who suffered during the Famine, or of those who were evicted in minor clearances after the Famine, such as the Derryveagh evictions in 1861. Two points, however, can be made about the Famine evictions. First, eviction accounted for only about 27 per cent of those who gave up agricultural holdings between 1847 and 1850; it accounted for an even smaller percentage of those who had only houses in the countryside — about 18 per cent. Secondly, the land vacated frequently went to other small farmers, often very small farmers as in the union of Kilrush. Farmers during the Land War may have liked to think of themselves as the victims of the Famine, but they were in fact often the legatees of those who were removed.

What about evictions in the post-Famine decades? Could one go as far as SoLOW and say that there were *too* few? Viewed as a traumatic experience, Irish tenants suffered eviction relatively infrequently compared with some of the other disasters suffered by individuals in Victorian society, which was characterised by abrupt transformations of status. In 1861, a relatively bad year, there were 1,092 evictions; in the same year, 203,422 people were admitted to workhouses; even assuming that all of those evicted went into the workhouses, they accounted for only 2·5 per cent of the workhouse population: the balance was accounted for by the rural and urban poor, whose combined numbers hardly exceeded that of the tenants. (It is also worth noting that agricultural labourers could suffer the equivalent of eviction with none of the formalities enjoyed by tenants, such as six months notice to quit.) Evictions were less frequent than industrial accidents in British factories: in 1861, one worker in every 200 in textile factories was injured — much more than the rate of eviction. Similarly one soldier in every 600 in the British army was flogged in 1861 — again higher than the rate of eviction.

Eviction was predominantly a form of insolvency; although there were exceptions, most evicted tenants were heavily in arrears. Did evictions represent a high rate of insolvency? In Prussia where peasant ownership was the predominant form of landownership, there were 33,972 forced sales of peasant properties between 1858 and 1867; or one for every 64 holdings. In Ireland in the same period there were 8,411 evictions, or one for every 72 holdings — a slightly lower rate than in Prussia. The fact that there was a process analagous to eviction in Prussia, which was regarded as the tenurial elysium by those who advocated land reform in Ireland, suggests an important point: some form of eviction is inseparable from private property. Even if the three Fs had been granted in the 1850s, or if peasant proprietary had been established, farmers would have suffered either eviction or forced sales: the comparison with Prussia suggests that the landlord-tenant system may at this period have actually protected tenants from insolvency.

The significance of the 16,579 agrarian outrages reported by the police between 1848 and 1880 is more difficult to assess than evictions, even when it is grasped that only 40 per cent were caused by landlord-tenant disputes. (Agrarian crime accounted for only about 10 per cent of *all* serious crime; only 4 per cent of crime, therefore, was caused by landlord-tenant disputes.) The land system caused crime, but it was only one of the criminogenic agencies at work: disputes within families and disputes between tenants and their neighbours, including sub-tenants, caused the bulk of agrarian crime. Disputes between tenants about inheritance, trespassing, sub-letting and competition for vacant farms generated 4,807 crimes, compared with 4,641 caused by rents and evictions. Considering the number of transactions between landlords and tenants that could easily cause friction — 400,000 rent increases, 1,000,000 rent collections annually, 80,000 evictions and probably 400,000 threats of eviction between 1848 and 1880 — this was not impressive. A change in the law relating to the inheritance of tenants' property, for example, might have reduced crime more than the introduction of the 3 Fs. Looked at from its most serious aspect, the interaction of 500,000 tenants and their landlords caused about one or, at most, two homicides a year; but compared with the British coal-mining industry, for example, where 1,000 miners (out of a workforce of 300,000 in the 1850s) died annually in accidents, the Irish land system was relatively benign.

Finally, what was the significance of the tenant right custom? It was a remarkable institution, working without legal support until 1870, and suggesting a high degree of co-operation between landlords and tenants. Whether it made rural Ulster prosperous is not so clear, for there were other possible explanations for the relative prosperity of the northern province: the cultivation of flax, the existence of good markets for agricultural produce in Belfast, the inherent quality of the soil, and the intensive application of labour on farms smaller than the national average may have had as much effect as tenant right. What is clear, however, is that Ulster counties were relatively free from agrarian crime, although some southern counties like Wicklow and Dublin were equally peaceful. Between 1858 and 1878, for example, only two northern landlords and their servants were involved in homicides, and both were in one county, Donegal.

In one respect the traditional picture of Irish landlordism was fairly accurate: Irish landlords did not invest in their estates as lavishly as was common in Britain. The social significance of this was probably more important than its economic effects, for it is doubtful if the sort of improvements made in England would have been of much use in Ireland. By not investing, however, Irish landlords missed an opportunity to justify their existence as great landed proprietors, for re-investing rents was the one way of binding tenants to landlords that was available to great estates in the nineteenth century. By spending on improvements, even useless ones, landlords could redistribute agricultural incomes, help smaller farmers, encourage efficiency and obedience to estate rules, and give tenants a lift in bad years. There was much that was inappropriate in the best contemporary practice, but many real opportunities existed in Ireland: drainage (which could be done efficiently only by landlords);

house building, especially for small tenants and labourers; the inspection and marketing of butter; funds for insurance and loans.

The essential weakness of the land system was not its oppressiveness but the fact that landlords became less useful to tenants as the century progressed. By the mid-nineteenth century landlords had ceased to be the dominant sources of law and order in their localities. The new constabulary, established in 1836, for example, was not under their control — as Sir Thomas Larcom noted: 'The head remains to them, but the arm is moved by the government, to a great extent independently of them'. As government patronage declined, landlords had less to give (in any case the period 1846-74 was dominated by Liberal governments, and most landlords were Tories). Even the repeal of the Corn Laws in 1846, although not affecting Ireland as much as Britain, was an indication of the landed interest's inability to maintain agriculture's privileged position. Not only did traditional sources of power decline, but landlords failed to exploit new ones (as well as the obvious one of estate investment): banks, railways, and shops were potential sources of power that landlords failed to exploit, unlike other dominant groups in the Victorian world. Another area of failure was rent collection, for although rents were relatively low, landlords failed to demonstrate that fact in practice. (A comparison with the state, which relatively painlessly extracted large sums from the people, is relevant: first, much of the state's revenue was levied indirectly; secondly, for the most part, payment was based on ability to pay and responded to fluctuations of economic fortune; thirdly, the only direct taxes on land which were analogous to rents were extracted in a systematic and equitable way.) By the 1870s, therefore, landlords existed on the fringes of rural society, but extracted large sums of money from it by using cumbersome legal techniques. Also, they had become dependent on a system of law enforcement that was public and not under their control.

WHAT CAUSED THE LAND WAR?

A visitor to Ireland in the mid-1870s would have found it difficult to foresee the Land War of 1879-82. Agrarian crime and evictions were running at low levels; even the composition of agrarian crime was changing, for family disputes were becoming more important as landlord-tenant disputes declined. Also the Land Act of 1870, in spite of the criticisms made of it, was having a considerable effect on estate management, and tenants were in a better position than they had been in the 1850s and 1860s. Some contemporaries might have perceived a decisive change in the nature of landlord-tenant relations when the landlords suffered a major electoral defeat in 1874, worse than in 1852 and 1868. One of the less obvious achievements of Irish landlords was their retention of electoral power over the new electorate created in 1850 — in spite of the Tenant League and clerical influence. It is true that landlords who wanted political office had to be more whiggish and more prone to please priests and Presbyterian ministers than landlords as a class were disposed to be. The bulk of Irish landlords were certainly as Tory as English landlords, but some lip-service to non-Tory policies was necessary, even in Ulster; such lip-service, when judiciously rendered, enabled landlords to play a major part in electoral politics in all general elections between 1852 and 1874. The great Liberal victory in 1868 had been a setback, and the disestablishment of the Irish church and the Land Act of 1870 had been regarded as defeats by many landlords; but 1874 was different and had more pronounced stigmata of defeat. First, the number of M.P.s who were landlords fell sharply — from 73 in 1868 to only 52 in 1874; secondly, the electoral triumph of Home Rule, precarious though it was, marked a shift in popular loyalties rather beyond the point that many landlords could go; finally, the defeat of 1868 had been part of an electoral swing throughout the United Kingdom, which saw the defeat of landlords and Tories everywhere, especially in Wales; but in 1874 the tide turned and Tories won their greatest electoral victory for over a generation — except in Ireland.

Yet the political setback of 1874 was less important than it appeared; for one thing, the local power of the landlords was not seriously threatened: they still controlled grand juries, poor-law boards and the magistracy; also a Tory administration in Dublin Castle for six years was a reassuring thing for a generation that had not seen a long period of Tory rule since the fall of Peel. Those more intimately connected with Irish land, however, might have been struck by more fundamentally alarming developments than the loss of electoral power. In the 1870s, for instance, the gap between actual and potential rents was greater than ever before; in a very real sense, the tenants' greatest victory took place before the Land War even started. Also, the Land Act of 1870 concentrated the land question in a way that was potentially dangerous for landlords; for the tenants, having now got about half of the three Fs, progress to full fixity of tenure became easier.

The Land War was one of the most important events of the nineteenth century, ranking with the campaign for Catholic emancipation in political history. The wave of agitation, violence and political brokerage that began in the spring of 1879 and ended in the summer of 1882 is not an easy process to describe. It was not a war in the sense of having discrete campaigns; nor was it decisively climactic in any of its characteristic forms of conflict; nor did it have definite turning-points except, possibly, the willingness of Parnell to become president of the Land League in 1879, or Gladstone's decision to grant the three Fs in 1881. Agrarian outrages increased to unprecedented levels and evictions reached levels not recorded since the early 1850s, but their peaks did not coincide: the former reached their highest level in the winter of 1880, and the latter only in the spring of 1882. Certain events, however, stand out even if they cannot be seen as turning-points: in 1879 the meetings in Connaught in the spring and summer, the 'negotiations' involving Parnell, Davitt and Devoy, and the formation of the Irish National Land League in October; in 1880 the spread of the Land League to the whole country, the general election in March, and the failure of the government's Compensation for Disturbance (Ireland) Bill in August; in 1881 the coercion crisis in the parliamentary

party, the Land Law (Ireland) Act in August, the arrest of
Parnell, the issuing of the No Rent Manifesto and the proclama-
tion of the Land League as 'an unlawful and criminal associa-
tion' in October; in 1882 the movement ran down, a process
marked by the Kilmainham 'treaty' and the Arrears of Rent
(Ireland) Act, passed in August. Although violence marked all
stages of the Land War particular episodes helped to intensify
an impression of deep disorder: the murder of Lord Mount-
morres in September 1880 coincided with a growing wave of
agrarian crime, and the Maamstrasna murders in August 1882
seemed to demonstrate the ineradicable violence of rural society
even when the Land War seemed effectively over.

The search for the causes of the Land War is a central
concern of historians, but this search can seriously distort the
past. First, every weakness of the land system can be made to
contribute to the *dénouement* of 1879, regardless of importance,
or even actual existence,· and the Land War becomes the
culmination of a long historical process. Secondly, the strengths
of the land system can be ignored — the fact that it put the
majority of tenants in a privileged position in rural society, and
that for all its ramshackle nature it had the strengths of famili-
arity and usage. Thirdly, the nature of the Land War itself can
become distorted if it is assumed that rural Ireland was like a
volcano, the opening of even the smallest fissure on which would
release an irrepressible flow of lava. This is a great exaggera-
tion, for agrarian crime before 1879 shows that the land system
generated relatively little friction, considering the number of
transactions between landlords and tenants; also before 1879,
the most important aspect of rural society was the absence of
institutional resistance to landlordism — Irish tenants were much
less organized, for example, than English farm labourers. Nor
was the Land War itself sensational as a *jacquerie:* there were
67 agrarian homicides between 1879 and 1882, but few of these
involved landlords and agents; agrarian crime increased
dramatically above pre-1879 levels, but much of this was
caused by threatening letters, a sort of literary compromise
between talk and violence. Nor does the history of the Land
War suggest a volcanic avalanche: the League spread slowly from

Mayo, and the 'war' did not really begin until the winter of 1880; nor did the mass of the tenantry ever come near a rent strike, for only about 25 per cent of rents due between 1879 and 1882 were not paid; most remarkable of all, the petty sessions courts, presided over by landlords, continued to function normally — about a million cases were disposed of during the four years 1879-82. Paul BEW's *Land and the National Question in Ireland, 1858-82* shows clearly the tentative nature of the tenants' alliance, the tensions that developed within the League as it expanded, and the limited tactics at its disposal, for the League seems to have been anything but monolithic, disciplined and inexorable. In fact the war was little more than a series of spasmodic skirmishes, and it is debatable whether landlords were really defeated by the Land League. For one thing, a staggering 11,215 evictions took place between 1879 and 1882 (twice as many as during the previous agricultural depression of the early 1860s); secondly, if landlords found it difficult to collect their rents, the Land League found it almost impossible to prevent the tenants from paying some rent. To say that the result was a draw is to exaggerate the success of the League.

In spite of such qualifications, however, the search for the causes of the Land War remains important. Historians writing in the 1930s had no doubt: POMFRET saw the Land War as the culmination of the tensions created by predatory landlordism, exacerbated by agricultural depression. On the whole this explanation was accepted by historians until the 1970s — with one important exception. In 1949 T. W. MOODY published his important article on the 'New Departure', describing the complex coincidence of forces represented by Devoy, Davitt and Parnell. According to Moody the New Departure was not an alliance, none of the protagonists quite understood the reservations of the others, and the Land War was not the fulfilment of their vague plans; rather the actual course of events transformed the intentions of the architects of the New Departure to such an extent that the recreation of their intentions in 1878 is extremely difficult — a task ultimately performed by MOODY with consummate skill in his monumental *Davitt and Irish*

Revolution (1982). The importance of MOODY's work was that
is dispelled the idea that the coincidence of agrarian discontent
and political leadership was inevitable, or even obvious — in spite
of the frequently repeated quotation from Fintan Lalor that
political independence could be joined to the land question like
a railway train coupled to an engine. MOODY, however, in his
article, although not in his biography of Davitt, presumed the
existence of an unstable land system and the importance of the
agricultural depression of 1879. (If anything, he exaggerated
the seriousness of the depression, assuming that potato losses
in 1877 and 1878 alone amounted to £12 millions, an
astronomical sum compared with the actual annual value of Irish
agricultural output.)

Until the 1970s the New Departure, the weaknesses of the
land system, and the agricultural depression of 1879 were the
tripartite explanation of the Land War accepted in the best
historical circles. Then came the changes in scholarship relating
to landlordism. How, it was asked, could the land system have
caused the Land War if most landlords were not harsh? Also
the effects of the agricultural depression were questioned. First,
it was clear that Ireland, or rather most of Ireland, had not
suffered as badly as was thought. T. W. FLETCHER, for example, argued that livestock producing areas of Great Britain,
like Ireland, were less depressed than tillage areas. Secondly,
DONNELLY pointed out that there had been as serious an
agricultural depression in Ireland in the early 1860s, unaccom-
panied by a land war.

Two ingenious explanations have been put forward to
explain why the Land War broke out in 1879. DONNELLY
in *Land and People of Cork* argued that the Land War was
caused by 'rising expectations' created by prosperity; the
occurrence of the Land War in 1879 and not in 1861 he
explained by the duration of the prosperity: that preceding 1861
had not lasted long enough to create rising expectations, while
that preceding 1879 had. CLARK argued that the agricultural
depressions did not matter, for at most they caused only anger
among the tenants; a rebellion such as the Land War required
not only anger but leadership and organization as well. (CLARK

was consciously influenced by Charles Tilly's *La Vendée;* he was perhaps unaware that his concern with leadership echoed Bram Stoker's Count Dracula — fiction's most predatory landlord — who had once asked 'What good are peasants without a leader?')* According to CLARK the leadership in 1879 was provided by townsmen — shopkeepers, journalists and publicans — who were over-represented among active Land Leaguers. The reason why they took the lead was simple: the tenants owed them money. The Land War, therefore, was a struggle between two groups of creditors, trying to recover debts caused by economic depression: landlords trying to recover arrears and shopkeepers trying to have their bills paid.

Neither of these explanations is without difficulty, not because historians are more given to disputatiousness than other scholars, but because of the exigencies of the problem itself. Historians almost always have problems with causation. On the one hand, the neatly packaged monocausal explanation is intellectually attractive; on the other, the events studied usually demand an untidy eclecticism. DONNELLY and CLARK may rightly feel that they have concentrated the minds of their colleagues, but their only reward may be the unwelcome one of seeing their apparently water-tight cases disintegrating as research progresses.

Also the explanations themselves, as they are presented, offer problems. DONNELLY, for example, does not actually demonstrate that expectations were rising; he shows that prosperity was increasing, and rising expectations are merely inferred from that. It is possible, however, that many farmers merely hoarded their new wealth: bank deposits in the 1860s and 1870s certainly suggest that many farmers were saving. (The expansion of banking supports DONNELLY's argument, although he does not mention it.) The greatest weakness of DONNELLY's case, however, is the timing of his revolution of rising expectations. If the seven years of prosperity before 1861 did not increase expectations, why did the fifteen between 1864 and 1878 have such a profound effect, expecially since they were not

---

* Stoker's first essay on predatory landlordism was a textbook entitled *The Duties of Clerks of Petty Sessions in Ireland* (Dublin, 1879).

without interruption, with setbacks in 1867 and 1872? Much the same objection can be made to CLARK'S case. There were in Ireland in 1861 52,000 townsmen of the kind regarded as important by Clark; by 1881 this number had increased to 61,000. What is magical about this increase? Why did not a crisis, similar to that of 1879-80, develop in 1861 in those areas where townsmen were powerful? Carlow in 1861, for example, had 10 townsmen for each thousand of population; Mayo in 1881 had 6: why did Carlow not rebel in 1861? Nor was there anything new about leadership by shopkeepers in 1879, for the idea had been seized on by Gavan Duffy in the 1850s.

The one incontestable fact that emerges is that 1879 was the only year of serious agricultural depression that found a united and powerful political leadership, ready to exploit agrarian discontent. In 1861, for example, there was not the same interest in the land: the Fenians were not closely connected with tenants, and Stephens at least did not see them as potential revolutionaries; the alternative leadership, George Henry Moore and The O'Donoghue had other ideas, such as the formation of a national volunteer force. Also the leadership in 1879 was remarkably impressive: Davitt and Parnell were formidable figures compared with any of their predecessors, except possibly Daniel O'Connell. Lucas, Gavan Duffy and McKnight, the leaders of the tenants in 1851-2, were not as impressive, or even as well known; potential leaders of an agrarian movement in the 1860s, such as Vincent Scully and John Francis Maguire, were not in the same class as Parnell and Davitt.

The timing of the New Departure was crucial: it established a potential alliance and organization before the worst of the agricultural depression occurred, that is, before the winter of 1879. In the 1850s, on the other hand, the Tenant League was established just as things were getting better: its organizers were building barriers against a receding tide, while Davitt and Parnell built against a powerful, incoming tide. Also if the New Departure had occurred earlier or later than it did, it might not have achieved so much; if earlier, the protagonists might have seen through each other sooner; if later, other leaders, more intimately connected with farmers, might have entrenched themselves and organized a different kind of agitation. There is the fact too that the land question had a potentially greater share of political attention in 1879 than it had ever had before. In the early 1850s there were many grievances in the countryside: poor-law rates, for example, were as unpopular as rents; also there was an embarrassment of panaceas to assist the economy — protection, lower taxation, as well as the three Fs. Above all, there were other powerful issues to distract attention from the land: the Durham letter and the Ecclesiastical Titles bill, for example. In the early 1860s the distractions were even stronger: the Fenians, the American Civil War, the invasion of Sicily-Naples by Garibaldi and the invasion of the Papal States by Sardinia, and even the cattle plague of 1865, which made the tenants dependent on strong, resolute government. By the 1870s, however, politics had changed: the Church of Ireland had been disestablished, the Pope had finally been evicted from the Patrimony of St. Peter, the Fenians had revealed their incapacity in 1867, and the amnesty movement had petered out; only the superficially successful issue of Home Rule existed as a serious rival to the land question. According to Walter Bagehot, the British electoral system was like an American forest: as trees were felled, new growth began. In the 1870s, therefore, the Irish political forest was in an interesting state of transition: Gladstone had hewed away a generation of discontent by disestablishing the Irish Church; he had marked out new lines of growth by his Land Act in 1870. There was nothing inevitable, however, about the New Departure, and it is difficult in retrospect to grasp how powerful were the arguments against identifying nationalism with an agrarian movement. First, the tenants had not shown themselves very powerful agitators: their adherence to the Tenant League in the 1850s had been temporary; the amount of institutional resistance to landlordism since then had been paltry — at most a few dozen tenants' protection societies; the idea that there was a great reservoir of discontent was obvious to few before 1879. Secondly, a significant number of Fenians, nationalist politicians and bishops were opposed to taking up the land question; even Parnell, after all, was slow to commit himself. It is only when the New Departure is seen against this background that the creative success of Davitt, Dèvoy and Parnell can be appreciated.

One further consideration emphasizes the accidental nature of what happened in 1879. What would have happened in Ireland if war had broken out between Britain and Russia in 1878? There is nothing so forgettable in history as wars that did not happen, yet a war in the Balkans in 1878 would have had profound effects on Ireland: the price of agricultural commodities would have held firm; the bad harvests of 1879 would have been mitigated by higher prices; and the attention of the Fenians would have been attracted to international politics. (The land meeting at Knock, County Mayo, in June 1879, gave a picture of what involvement in the Land War implied for Fenians: attacks on landlords and Archdeacon Kavanagh were interspersed with invocations of the Zulus and Afghans.)

In a deep sense the leadership of Parnell and Davitt was crucial. One of the mysteries of Irish rural life before 1879 was the absence of institutional organization in the countryside: farmers had few opportunities to learn how to organize, to set up committees, to appoint leaders and to evolve realistic aims. Clark's emphasis on the gradual development of 'collective action' really misses the point: there had been very little collective action, except political movements that were peripheral and remote from the tenants. Rural society was ramified rather than nucleated; collective action was often implicit rather than explicit in its aims, and informal in organization. Permanent, formal activity was rare: there were few friendly societies or insurance clubs, and most Irish tenants did not belong to churches with self-government involving the laity—as in Wales, for example. Mobilizing such a society was not easy; clear, simple personal leadership was required, something easily identified with—faces rather than principles.

THE LAND WAR AND THE LAND QUESTION

In retrospect the Land War seems a decisive stage in the history of landlord-tenant relations. The main achievement of the Land League, the Land Act of 1881, which established a system of dual ownership in which rents were fixed by special tribunals, eventually reconciled the landlords to land purchase. Also it created an alliance between nationalists and tenants that endured for decades, and went a long way to securing self-government for Ireland. From the nationalists' point of view, the timing of events was fortunate. If Parnell and Davitt had not seized the leadership of the agrarian movement in 1879, it is unlikely that nationalists would ever have secured mass electoral support; without their leadership, the agrarian crisis would have produced its own leadership, preoccupied and torn by conflicting agrarian interests; or it might have produced no leadership at all, like the crisis in the early 1860s. Even if the tenants had produced a unified movement, strong enough to survive the crises of 1879-82, it is difficult to see how such a movement could have captured the labourers when they were enfranchised in 1885. Without the New Departure and Parnellism, nationalism would probably have split into a number of impotent fragments: constitutional home rulers who would have been drawn into the orbit of the new Liberal government after 1880; ageing Fenians, waiting for a European war that was only a remote possibility as long as Bismarck controlled Germany; idealist successors of George Henry Moore and William O'Neill Daunt who might have consoled themselves by vindicating the rights of Ireland within the new literary movement.

The profound effects of the New Departure and the Land War were displayed within a few years of 1882 when in 1885 the great electoral victory of Home Rule and the Land Purchase Act set the scene for the next generation. The system of dual ownership became firmly established, and co-existed with the very halting progress of land purchase: it took a long succession of statutes between 1885 and 1909 to entice the majority of Irish tenant farmers to become owner occupiers. Yet the short-term effects of the Land War should not be exaggerated. The Land Act of 1881 did not have dramatic effects; during its first ten years, only £1·4 million was taken off Irish rents. (It is doubtful if these figures underestimate the reduction in rents, for rentals show the same fall.) It is even arguable that landlords were better off with the act than without it, for it stabilized rents; if rents had fallen in line with agricultural output, for example, their fall would have been greater—to some extent, therefore, landlords actually recovered some of the financial ground they had lost in the 1870s. Some landlords were, however, embarrass- ed by a fall in their incomes, expecially those already in debt, as CURTIS has shown. But it cannot be argued that the Land War broke the spirit of the landlords: the wave of evictions between October 1881 and the middle of 1882, probably the worst since the Famine clearances, showed that many landlords had reserves of toughness that might have surprised observers who knew only the Ireland of the 1870s. It has been argued that the Land War irreparably damaged the spirit of deference that had sustained the land system before 1879—that tenants stopped lifting their hats to landlords. This is a doubtful argument; for one thing, there is not much evidence one way or the other—unfortunately the R.I.C. did not keep statistics of hat lifting. What little evidence there is suggests there was no revolution in manners: testimonials to landed families on occasions such as the heir's majority continued; the petty sessions continued to play an important part in local law enforcement right up to the end of British rule (and for longer in Northern Ireland); local government was dominated by landlords until 1898, although they began to lose control of the poor law boards in the 1880s. Finally, it is worth remembering that the system established in 1881 lasted for over thirty years: it may have been unsatisfactory, but Parliament found it difficult to persuade tenants to buy their farms without considerable inducements.

The tenants did not emerge from the Land War with many new skills in organization and resistance. If anything, the Land

War created divisions and brought home the dangers of resistance. Between 1879 and 1883 14,600 tenants were evicted, which was almost one in thirty and more than had been evicted in the previous twenty years. The tenants' victory had been won at a cost; if there had been no resistance to landlords in 1879-81 and if the crisis of 1879-82 had passed like that of 1861-2, there might have been 3 or 4,000 evictions (as there were in 1861-2): the difference between what happened and what might have happened was 10,000 evictions, which was one of the costs of the Land Act of 1881. (It is also remarkable that the number of evictions, even after 1882, in spite of the Land Act and the Arrears Act, remained high by pre-1879 standards, suggesting a new harshness in landlord-tenant relations.) The depression that began in 1885 was probably worse that that of 1879-80, but it did not lead to a similar outburst; for the Plan of Campaign, while it was better organized than the Land War, fell far short of a great popular attack on landlordism, and by 1892 it was by no means clear that the tenants had won. It is remarkable that Irish tenants, under the impact of two major depressions in agriculture, did not organize more effectively, for neither the Land League nor the Plan of Campaign compared in effectiveness with industrial trade unions.

If the Land War was a turning point in the history of the land question, it was not only because of the achievements of the Land League; for the period 1879-86 coincided with profound changes in the fortunes of agriculture. The crisis of 1879 was not a temporary setback in a rising market, like that of 1861-2; it was in fact the beginning of a long recession in European agriculture that lasted into the twentieth century. Although there was some recovery in the early 1880s, prices fell sharply in 1885-6, to points even lower than in 1879. These two crises were like a hinge in the history of nineteenth-century agriculture: on the one side prosperity interrupted by temporary setbacks, and on the other, stagnation occasionally disturbed by short periods of prosperity. It was the changing fortunes of agriculture as much as the Land War that undermined landlordism, for land ceased to be an attractive investment, and land purchase offered the prospect of exchanging land for money.

If the crisis of 1879-80 had been temporary, the Land Act of 1881 could easily have served as a new land code, leaving landlords in a strong position where they would have been forced to do nothing that they had not done before 1879; in fact the act might have given them some interesting new powers, such as the right to have the value of tenant right fixed by the courts (a power that was useful only in a rising market); it might have forced them to manage their estates more effectively; above all it might have introduced some useful tension into the relationship between landlords and tenants, binding them together and engrossing them in constructive conflict. Without the lift of rising prices, however, the Land Act of 1881 was not so important, except in killing the Land League and stabilizing rents.

At most, then, the Land War was a stage in the dismantling of landlordism, comparable with the electoral victory of Home Rule in 1885, the First World War, the War of Independence and partition. Moreover the decline of the gentry was not an inevitable result of the destruction of landlordism, for it was envisaged that they would survive the sale of their tenanted land. By 1914 three-quarters of occupiers were buying out their landlords, mostly under the great acts of 1903 and 1904, which directly initiated the decisive decline of tenancy and led to the transfer in ownership of about nine million acres to the occupiers. In the 1920s, in both parts of Ireland, land purchase was made compulsory and the remaining tenanted land was taken from the landlords. The most striking sign of the decline of landlordism, the disappearance of the gentry from the countryside, was only evident from that decade: by the 1970s hardly one quarter of the mansion houses of the 1870s were lived in by descendants of nineteenth-century landed families.

Landlords had remained important in the countryside after 1881, and even after their metamorphosis under the land purchase acts. They played a part in the co-operative movement started by one of their own number, Horace Plunkett; they were connected with the Irish literary movement through George Moore and Lady Gregory, and were benignly immortalized in the works of Edith Somerville and Martin Ross; they became firmly entrenched in the great Conservative alliance that dominated British politics from 1886 to 1906, one of whose first fruits was Arthur Balfour's chief secretaryship (1887-92) during which landlords and government were more closely combined than they had been for forty years; they remained politically important in Ulster where they led the Unionists after 1886 and provided three prime ministers of Northern Ireland between 1921 and 1971. History was kind to the Irish landlords in their decline, and their going was unmarred by great acts of ineptitude: they produced no Franz von Papen to usher in a Hitler, nor a Claus von Stauffenberg who failed to usher him out.

*   *   *

Was the land question as important as it seemed to nineteenth-century Irishmen? There is no doubt that it gave nationalists an important opportunity to establish themselves between 1879 and 1882. But it did not dominate politics before 1879, for it had to compete with other issues such as the disestablishment of the Irish church. Nor was it a barrier to agricultural progress, for farmers prospered before they were given security of tenure. If landlordism had been abolished in the early 1850s, most of the benefits would have been enjoyed by larger tenants, and smaller tenants and labourers would have gained relatively less; if the three Fs had been granted in the 1850s, or even in 1870, rents might actually have been higher and evictions more frequent, although sensational incidents like the Derryveagh evictions could not have occurred. As the number of agricultural labourers declined, the tenurial relationship between landlords and tenants became more important; but it was rivalled by a new one, the link between debtors and creditors. In the early 1870s, for example, for every civil bill ejectment process issued, there were fifty ordinary processes for debt.

The real importance of the land question was perhaps less obvious. Because of the well established obsession with landlord-tenant relations, and the events of 1879-82, the whole issue of Irish land came to be viewed exclusively in terms of ownership and occupation. Against the drama of evictions and agrarian crime, the minutiae of agricultural improvement and rural organization seemed dull; against the contending claims of landlords and tenants, the claims of other groups — landless labourers, taxpayers, and city people who wanted access to land — seemed less pressing. As a result, when landlordism was abolished, it was replaced by a highly private system of owner-ship. Public control was limited to the modestly exercised powers of the Land Commission; the landlords as centres of power were not replaced; farming became confined to those who inherited land, with some exceptions; physical access, even to stretches of beach, became a matter of private arrangement. Thus despite the Land League's campaign, the 'land for the people' did not lead to the establishment of great national forests, to areas of common land, or even to public footpaths. Above all, the land ceased to be a source of revenue; in the 1860s, for example, 25 per cent of total Irish revenue was raised directly by taxes on land; in the course of the twentieth century, the expiry of land purchase annuities, the abolition of local government rates, and the growth of central government's assistance to agriculture have transformed the land into a net receiver of public revenue.

SELECT BIBLIOGRAPHY

Since the ownership and occupation of land touched so many aspects of Irish life, primary sources are rich and copious, covering the whole range of historical evidence from folk lore to government statistics. Although a completely comprehensive study of land might include such diverse sources as diocesan archives (L.P. Curtis, for example, has used the papers of the Representative Church Body to study landlords' indebtedness) and the auction catalogues of private libraries (showing the books on land management used by Irish landlords), the most immediately useful are rather more limited: estate papers and accounts; parliamentary papers; pamphlets; newspapers; registered and unregistered papers in the State Paper Office, Dublin; transcriptions of deeds in the Registry of Deeds, Dublin; valuation records in the Valuation Office, Ely Place, Dublin and in the Public Record Office of Northern Ireland. The main collections of estate papers are in the National Library of Ireland, the Public Record Office of Ireland, and the Public Record Office of Northern Ireland. The most complete set of parliamentary papers in Ireland is in the library of Trinity College, Dublin; the best collection of newspapers in Ireland is in the National Library, and R. D. C. Black's *A Catalogue of Pamphlets on Economic Subjects Published between 1750 and 1900 and now Housed in Irish Libraries* (Belfast and New York, 1969) gives details of the location of most of the pamphlets relevant to the land question.

There is now a considerable body of secondary works, of which a selection is given below. It is important, however, to see the land question in a wide context, for many of the difficulties associated with Irish land are inseparable from any system of private ownership that permits partial alienation by mortgaging, leasing or sub-letting. Even the prevalence of great estates, the most obvious characteristic of landownership in nineteenth-century Ireland, was not peculiar to Ireland, or even to the British Isles. On the land system in the rest of the United

Kingdom, see F. M. L. Thompson, *English Landed Society in the Nineteenth Century* (London, 1963); G. E. Mingay (ed.), *The Victorian Countryside* (2 vols, London, 1981); David Howell, *Land and People in Nineteenth-Century Wales* (London 1978). On European landed elites generally, see David Spring (ed.), *European Landed Elites in the Nineteenth Century* (Baltimore and London, 1977) and Ralph Gibson and Martin Blinkhorn (eds), *Landownership and Power in Modern Europe* (London, 1991).

BELL, J[onathan]. 'The Improvement of Irish Farming Techniques since 1750: Theory and Practice'. In Patrick O'Flanagan, Paul Ferguson, Kevin Whelan (ed.), *Rural Ireland, 1600–1900: Modernization and Change* (Cork, 1987), 24–41.

—————— and WATSON, Mervyn. *Irish Farming. Implements and Techniques* 1750–1900 (Edinburgh, 1986).

BEW, Paul. *Land and the National Question in Ireland 1858–82* (Dublin, 1978)—deals mainly with the Land War, 1879–82.

—————— 'The Land League Ideal: Achievement and Contradictions'. In Drudy (ed.), op. cit., 77–92.

—————— and WRIGHT, Frank. 'The Agrarian Opposition in Ulster Politics, 1848–87'. In Clark and Donnelly (ed.), op. cit., 192–229.

BLACK, R. D. Collison. *Economic Thought and the Irish Question 1817–1870* (Cambridge, 1960)—describes contemporary thinking on landlordism, poor law, public works and emigration.

BOYLE, John W. 'A Marginal Figure: the Irish rural Labourer'. In Clarke and Donnelly (ed.), op. cit., 311–38.

BRADY, J. C. 'Legal Developments, 1801–79' in W. E. Vaughan (ed.), *A New History of Ireland*, vol. v, *Ireland under the Union, I, 1801-70* (Oxford, 1989), 451–81.

BUCKLEY, K. 'The Fixing of Rents by Agreement in County Galway, 1881–5', *Ir. Hist. Stud*, VII, 27 (Mar. 1951), 149–79.

BURN, W. L. 'Free Trade in Land: An Aspect of the Irish Question', *Trans. Royal Hist. Soc.*, 4th ser., XXXI (1949), 61–74.

CLARK, Samuel. 'The Social Composition of the Land League', *Ir. Hist. Stud.*, XVII, 68 (Sept. 1971), 447–69.

———— 'The Political Mobilization of Irish Farmers', *Canadian Review of Sociology and Anthropology*, XXII, 4, pt 2 (Nov. 1975), 483–99.

———— *Social Origins of the Irish Land War* (Princeton, 1979)— discusses the relationship between agrarian change and 'collective action' from the 1840s.

———— 'The Importance of Agrarian Classes: Agrarian Class Structure and Collective Action in Nineteenth-Century Ireland'. In Drudy (ed.), op. cit., 11–36.

———— 'Landlord Domination in Nineteenth-century Ireland', *UNESCO Yearbook on Peace and Conflict Studies, 1986* (Paris, 1988), 5–29.

———— and DONNELLY, James S., Jr. (ed.). *Irish Peasants. Violence and Political Unrest 1780–1914* (Manchester, 1983)—see articles by Bew and Wright, Boyle, Feingold and Walker.

CONNELL, K. H. 'The Land Legislation and Irish Social Life', *Econ. Hist. Rev.*, 2nd ser., XI, 1 (Aug. 1958), 1–7.

COLLINS, M. E. *The Land Question, 1879–1882* (Dublin, 1974).

CROTTY, Raymond. *Irish Agricultural Production: Its Volume and Structure* (Cork, 1966).

CURTIS, L. P. 'Incumbered Wealth: Landed Indebtedness in Post-Famine Ireland', *Amer. Hist. Rev.*, LXXXV, 2 (Apr. 1980), 332–67—shows how the disestablished Church of Ireland obeyed the divine command in Matt. 6:34 and lent its money to Irish landlords, and then to the Czar and the Sultan.

———— 'Stopping the Hunt, 1881–2: An Aspect of the Irish Land War'. In Philpin (ed.), op. cit., 349–402.

DEWEY, Clive. 'Celtic Agrarian Legislation and Celtic Revival: Historicist Implications of Gladstone's Irish and Scottish Land Acts, 1870–86', *Past & Present*, 64 (Aug. 1974), 30–70.

DONNELLY, James S., Jr. *Landlord and Tenant in Nineteenth-Century Ireland* (Dublin, 1973).

———— 'The Journals of Sir John Benn-Walsh Relating to the Management of his Irish Estates, 1823–64', *Cork Hist. Soc. Jn.*,

LXXIX, 230 (1974), 86–123; LXXX, 231 (1975), 15–42—fascinating account of the career of an absentee landlord.

———— *The Land and the People of Nineteenth-Century Cork. The Rural Economy and the Land Question* (London, 1975)—covers the period 1815–92, and is a most substantial study of the land question; for the 'crisis of rising expectations' see pp 249–50.

———— 'The Irish Agricultural Depression of 1859–64', *Ir. Econ. and Soc. Hist.,* III (1976), 33–54.

———— 'Production, Prices and Exports, 1846–51' and 'Landlords and Tenants' in W. E. Vaughan (ed.), *A New History of Ireland,* vol. v, *Ireland under the Union, I, 1801–70* (Oxford, 1989), 286–93, 332–49.

DRUDY, P. J. (ed.). *Ireland: Land, Politics and People* (Irish Studies 2: Cambridge, 1982)—see articles by Bew, Clark and Fitzpatrick.

DUFFY, Patrick. 'Irish Landholding Structure and Population in the Mid-Nineteenth Century', *Maynooth Review,* III, 2 (Dec. 1977), 3–27.

DUNLEAVY, J. C. and G. W. 'The Hidden Ireland of Irish Landlords: Manuscript Evidence of Oral Traditions', *Anglo-Irish Studies,* IV (1979), 47–58.

FEENEY, Patrick. 'Ballysaggart Estate: Eviction, Famine and Conspiracy', *Decies,* XXVII (autumn, 1984), 4–12.

FEINGOLD, W. L. 'The tenants' movement to capture the Irish poor law boards, 1877–1886', *Albion,* VII, 3 (Dec. 1975), 216–31.

———— *The First Hurrah: The Rise of Tenant Leadership in the Irish Localities, 1870–1886* (St Louis, Missouri, 1976).

———— 'Land League Power: The Tralee Poor-Law Election of 1881'. In Clark and Donnelly (ed.), 285–310.

———— *The Revolt of the Tenantry: The Transformation of Local Government in Ireland, 1872–1886,* (Boston, 1984).

FITZPATRICK, David. 'The Disappearance of the Irish Agricultural labourer, 1841–1921', *Ir. Econ. & Soc. Hist.,* VII (1980), 66–92.

FITZPATRICK, David. 'Class, Family and Rural Unrest in Nineteenth-Century Ireland'. In Drudy (ed.), op. cit., 37–75.

FLETCHER, T. W. 'The Great Depression of English Agriculture, 1873–1896', *Econ. Hist. Rev.*, 2nd ser., XIII, 3 (May 1961), 417–32.

GARVIN, Tom. 'Defenders, Ribbonmen and Others: Underground Political Networks in Pre-Famine Ireland'. In Philpin (ed.), op. cit., 219–63.

GOLDSTROM, J. M. 'Irish Agriculture and the Great Famine' In J. M. Goldstrom and L. A. Clarkson (ed.), *Irish Population, Economy and Society. Essays in Honour of the Late K. H. Connell* (Oxford, 1981), 155–71.

GUTTMAN, J. M. 'The Economics of Tenant Rights in Nineteenth-Century Irish Agriculture', *Economic Inquiry*, XVIII (July 1980), 408–24.

HAZELKORN, Ellen. 'Reconsidering Marx and Engels on Ireland', *Saothair*, IX (1983), 79–88.

HORN, Pamela L. R. 'The National Agricultural Labourers' Union in Ireland, 1873–9', *Ir. Hist. Stud.*, XVII, 67 (Mar. 1971), 340–352.

HOOKER, Elizabeth R. *Readjustments of Agricultural Tenure in Ireland*, (Chapel Hill, NC, 1938).

HOPPEN, K. Theodore. 'Landlords, Society and Electoral Politics in Mid-Nineteenth-Century Ireland', *Past & Present*, 75 (May 1977), 62–93—lively account of political complexities in the localities.

———— *Elections, Politics and Society in Ireland, 1832–1885* (Oxford, 1984).

———— 'Landownership and Power in Nineteenth-Century Ireland: the Decline of an Élite'. In Ralph Gibson and Martin Blinkhorn (ed.), *Landownership and Power in Modern Europe* (London, 1991), 164–80.

HUTTMANN, John P. 'The Impact of Land Reform on Agricultural Production in Ireland', *Agricultural History*, XLVI, 3 (July 1972), 353–68.

JORDAN, Donald. 'Merchants, "Strong Farmers" and Fenians: the Post-Famine Political Élite and the Irish Land War'. In Philpin (ed.), op. cit., 320–48.

KENNEDY, Liam. 'Regional Specialization, Railway Development and Irish Agriculture in the Nineteenth Century'. In J. M. Goldstrom and L. A. Clarkson (ed.), *Irish Population, Economy and Society* (Oxford, 1981), 173–93.

——— 'Farmers, Traders and Agricultural Politics in Pre-Independence Ireland'. In Clark and Donnelly (ed.), op. cit., 339–73.

——— 'The Rural Economy, 1820–1914'. In Liam Kennedy and Philip Ollerenshaw (ed.), *An Economic History of Ulster, 1820–1940* (Manchester, 1985), 1–61.

KIRKPATRICK, R. W. 'Origins and Development of the Land War in Mid-Ulster'. In F. S. L. Lyons and R. A. J. Hawkins (ed.), *Ireland under the Union: Varieties of Tension. Essays in Honour of T. W. Moody* (Oxford, 1980), 201–35.

LANE, P. G. 'The Encumbered Estates Court, Ireland, 1848–1849', *Eonomic and Social Review*, III (1972), 413–53.

——— 'The General Impact of the Encumbered Estates Act of 1849 on Counties Galway and Mayo', *Galway Archaeological and Historical Society Jn.*, XXXIII (1972-3), 44–74.

——— 'The Management of Estates by Financial Corporations in Ireland after the Famine', *Studia Hib.*, XIV, (1974), 67–89.

——— 'The Impact of the Encumbered Estates Court upon the Landlords of Galway and Mayo', *Galway Archaeological and Historical Society Jn.*, XXXVIII (1981-2), 45–58.

LEE, Joseph. 'The Land War'. In Liam de Paor (ed.), *Milestones in Irish History* (Dublin and Cork, 1986), 106–116.

LOWE, W. J. 'Landlord and Tenant on the Estate of Trinity College, Dublin, 1851–1903'. *Hermathena*, CXX (1976), 5–24.

MACCARTHY, Robert. *The Trinity College Estate 1800–1923. Corporate Management in an Age of Reform* (Dundalk, 1992).

McCOURT, Eileen. 'The Management of the Farnham Estates during the Nineteenth Century', *Breifne*, IV, (1975), 531–60.

McMINN, J. R. B. 'The Social and Political Structure of North Antrim in 1869', *Glynns*, X (1982), 11–22.

MAHON, Kevin and MCKEOWN, Thomas. 'Agrarian Disturbances around Crossmaglen, 1835–55', *Seanchas Ardmhacha*, IX, 2 (1979), 302–332; X, 1 (1981), 149–75; 2 (1982), 380–416.

MARNANE, Denis G. *Land and Violence. A History of West Tipperary from 1660* (Tipperary, 1985).

MOODY, T. W. *Davitt and Irish Revolution 1846–82* (Oxford, 1981)—the definitive account of the New Departure.

MORAN, Gerard P. 'Absentee Landlordism in Mayo in the 1870s', *Cathair na Mart*, II, 1 (1982), 30–52.

———— 'An Assessment of the Land League Meeting at Westport, 8 June 1879', *Cathair na Mart*, III, 1 (1983), 54–9.

———— 'Mayo and the General Election of 1874', *Cathair na Mart*, IV, 1 (1984), 69–73.

———— 'Famine and the Land War: Relief and Distress in Mayo, 1879–81', *Cathair na Mart*, V, 1 (1985), 54–66; VI, 1 (1986), 111–27.

MURPHY, Desmond. 'The Land War in Donegal, 1879–1891', *Donegal Annual*, 32 (1980), 476–86.

MURRAY, A. C. 'Nationality and Local Politics in Late Nineteenth-Century Ireland: the Case of County Westmeath', *Ir. Hist. Stud.*, XXV, 98 (Nov. 1986), 144–58.

———— 'Agrarian Violence and Nationalism in Nineteenth-Century Ireland: the Myth of Ribbonism', *Ir. Econ. & Soc. Hist.*, XIII (1986), 56–73.

NORMAN, E. R. *The Catholic Church and Ireland in the Age of Rebellion 1859–1873* (London, 1965)—interesting references to the land question in mid-century politics.

O'BRIEN, Conor Cruise. *Parnell and his Party 1880–90* (Oxford, 1957)—see pp 13–16 for decline in number of landlords elected to the house of commons in 1880.

Ó GRÁDA, Cormac. 'Agricultural Head Rents, Pre-Famine and Post-Famine', *Economic and Social Review*, V, 3 (Apr. 1974), 385–92.

———— 'The Investment Behaviour of Irish Landlords 1850–75: Some Preliminary Findings', *Agric. Hist. Rev.*, XXIII, 2 (1975), 139–55.

Ó GRÁDA, 'Irish Agricultural Output before and after the Famine', *The Journal of European Economic History*, XIII, 1 (spring 1984), 149–65.

———— *Ireland before and after the Famine. Explorations in Economic History, 1800–1925* (Manchester, 1988).

O'NEILL, T. P. 'The Irish Land Question, 1830–50', *Studies*, XLIV (autumn, 1955), 325–36.

ORRIDGE, A. W. 'Who supported the Land War? An Aggregate-Data Analysis of Irish agrarian Discontent, 1879–82', *Economic and Social Review*, XII, 3 (Apr. 1981), 203–33.

O'SHEA, James. *Priests, Politics and Society in Post-Famine Ireland: a Study of County Tipperary 1850–91* (Dublin and New Jersey, 1983).

PALMER, Norman Dunbar. *The Irish Land League Crisis* (New Haven, 1940).

PHELAN, M. M. 'Fr Thomas O'Shea and the Callan Tenant Protection Society', *Old Kilkenny Review*, n.s., II, 2 (1980), 49–58.

PHILPIN, C. H. E. (ed.). *Nationalism and Popular Protest in Ireland* (Cambridge, 1987).

POMFRET, John E. *The Struggle for Land in Ireland, 1800–1923* (Princeton, 1930).

PROUDFOOT, Lindsay. 'The Management of a Great Estate: Patronage, Income and Expenditure on the Duke of Devonshire's Irish Property, *c.* 1816–1891', *Ir. Econ. & Soc. Hist.*, XIII (1986), 32–55.

ROBINSON, Olive. 'The London Companies as Progressive Landlords in Nineteenth-Century Ireland', *Econ. Hist. Rev.*, 2nd ser., XV, 1 (Aug. 1962), 103–18.

———— 'The London Companies and Tenant Right in Nineteenth-Century Ireland', *Agric. Hist. Rev.*, XVIII (1970), 54–63.

SOCOLOFSKY, Homer E. *Landlord William Scully* (Kansas, 1979)—career of the Tipperary landlord who was wounded in a gun battle with his tenants in 1868.

SOLOW, B. L. *The Land Question and the Irish Economy 1870–1903* (Cambridge, Mass., 1971)—readable clear and concise.

———— 'A New Look at the Irish Land Question', *Economic & Social Review*, XII, 4 (July 1981), 301–314.

STEELE, David. *Irish Land and British Politics: Tenant Right and Nationality 1865–1870* (Cambridge, 1974)—a detailed account of the making of the Land Act of 1870.

TAYLOR, Lawrence J. 'The Priest and the Agent: Social Drama and Class Consciousness in the West of Ireland', *Comparative Studies in Society and History*, XXVII, 4 (Oct. 1985), 696–712.

THOMPSON, Francis. 'The Landed Classes, the Orange Order and the Anti-Land League Campaign in Ulster, 1880–81', *Éire-Ireland*, XXII, 1 (spring 1987), 102–21.

THORNLEY, David. *Isaac Butt and Home Rule (London, 1964)*—see pp 205–11 for landlords elected to the house of commons in 1868 and 1874.

TOWNSHEND, Charles. *Political Violence in Ireland. Government and Resistance since 1848* (Oxford, 1983).

TURNER, Michael. 'Towards an Agricultural Prices Index for Ireland, 1850–1914', *The Economic and Social Review*, XVIII, 2 (Jan. 1987), 123–36.

———— 'Output and Productivity in Irish agriculture from the famine to the great war', *Ir. Econ. & Soc. Hist.*, XVII (1990), 62–78.

VAUGHAN, W. E. *Landlords and Tenants in Mid-Victorian Ireland* (Oxford, 1993).

WALKER, Brian M. (ed.). *Parliamentary Election Results in Ireland 1801–1922* (Dublin, 1978).

———— 'The Land Question in Elections in Ulster, 1868–86'. In Clark and Donnelly (ed.), op. cit., 230–68.

———— *Ulster Politics. The Formative Years, 1868–86* (Belfast, 1989).

WINSTANLEY, Michael J. *Ireland and the Land Question, 1800–1922* (London and New York, 1984).

WHYTE, J. H. *The Independent Irish Party 1850–9* (London, 1958)—see pp 63–81 and 90–1 for a discussion of landlords' electoral power.

7 Day

University of Plymouth Library

Subject to status this item may be renewed
via your Voyager account

http://voyager.plymouth.ac.uk

Exeter tel: (01392) 475049
Exmouth tel: (01395) 255331
Plymouth tel: (01752) 232323